SMALL BITES, MIMOSAS AND MORE!

Publications International, Ltd.

Pictured on the front cover: Fruity Mimosa *(page 5)* and Simple Bruschetta *(page 97)*.

Pictured on the back cover *(clockwise from top)*: Mimosa *(page 14)*, Tipsy Chicken Wraps *(page 100)*, Creamy Mushroom Cups *(page 41)*, Micro Mini Stuffed Potatoes *(page 60)* and Bubbling Raspberry Cooler *(page 32)*.

ISBN: 978-1-68022-286-9

Library of Congress Control Number: 2015949888

Manufactured in China.

8 7 6 5 4 3 2 1

Microwave Cooking: Microwave ovens vary in wattage. Use the cooking times as guidelines and check for doneness before adding more time.

Preparation/Cooking Times: Preparation times are based on the approximate amount of time required to assemble the recipe before cooking, baking, chilling or serving. These times include preparation steps such as measuring, chopping and mixing. The fact that some preparations and cooking can be done simultaneously is taken into account. Preparation of optional ingredients and serving suggestions is not included.

Let's get social!
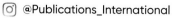
@Publications_International
@PublicationsInternational
www.pilbooks.com

TABLE OF CONTENTS

BREAK OUT THE BUBBLY

FRUITY MIMOSA •

2½ cups chilled strawberry-
 orange-banana juice
1 bottle (750 ml) chilled
 Champagne

Pour juice into eight champagne
flutes; top with champagne.

Makes 8 servings

. . . .

PINEAPPLE MIMOSA

¼ cup pink sanding sugar
1 bottle (750 ml) champagne
 or sparkling apple cider,
 chilled
¼ cup DOLE® Pineapple Juice
¼ cup blood orange juice or
 orange juice

• **Dip** rims of champagne flutes
or other glasses in water. Dip
again into sanding sugar.

• **Divide** champagne, pineapple
juice and blood orange juice
among 4 flutes.

Makes 4 servings

POMEGRANATE MIMOSA

2 cups chilled pomegranate juice

1 bottle (750 ml) chilled champagne

Pomegranate seeds (optional)

Pour pomegranate juice into eight champagne flutes; top with champagne. Garnish with pomegranate seeds.

Makes 8 servings

GINGER-PINEAPPLE SPRITZER

2 cups pineapple juice
1 tablespoon chopped
   crystallized ginger
1 cup chilled champagne
   Pineapple wedges (optional)

1. Combine pineapple juice and ginger in small saucepan; bring to a simmer over medium heat. Pour into small pitcher; cover and refrigerate 8 to 24 hours.

2. Strain juice mixture; discard ginger. Gently stir champagne into juice mixture. Serve over ice. Garnish with pineapple wedges.

Makes 4 servings

TIP: For a fun and festive holiday beverage, swap out the pineapple juice for cranberry juice.

MULLED RASPBERRY MOSAS

16 fresh **or** thawed frozen raspberries

1⅓ cups V8 Splash® Tropical Blend Juice, chilled

1 cup champagne **or** seltzer water, chilled

1. Place **4** raspberries in **each** of **4** fluted champagne glasses. Mash them lightly with a fork.

2. Pour ⅓ **cup** juice and ¼ **cup** champagne into **each** glass. Stir. Serve immediately.

Makes 4 servings

PREP TIME: 5 minutes
TOTAL TIME: 5 minutes

KIR

½ ounce crème de cassis
   (black currant liqueur)
¾ cup chilled dry white wine

Pour crème de cassis into wine glass; top with white wine.

Makes 1 serving

KIR ROYALE: Replace white wine with chilled champagne or dry sparkling wine; serve in champagne glass.

WATERMELON REFRESHER

6 cups ripe seedless
    watermelon chunks

¼ cup lemon juice

1 cup chilled champagne

    Berry-filled ice cubes
    (optional)

1. Place watermelon in blender; process in two batches until smooth. Pour into sieve and strain. Chill juice, if desired.

2. Combine 3 cups watermelon juice and lemon juice in medium pitcher. Gently stir in champagne. Serve over ice, if desired.

Makes 4 servings

ICY MIMOSAS

- 3 cups frozen Tropic Ice, crushed (recipe follows)
- 3 cups chilled champagne
- 6 whole strawberries

1. Prepare Tropic Ice.

2. Spoon ½ cup crushed Tropic Ice into each of six glasses; top with ½ cup champagne. Garnish with strawberry.

Makes 6 servings

TROPIC ICE

- 4 cups tropical fruit juice, such as pineapple, orange and banana
- 1 can (12 ounces) ginger ale
- ¾ cup frozen white grape juice concentrate
- ½ cup dry white wine (see Note)

1. Combine juice, ginger ale, juice concentrate and wine in large resealable freezer bag. Seal bag; freeze overnight or until frozen.

2. To use, pound bag with meat mallet to break up ice. Store remaining mixture in freezer until needed. Freeze leftovers up to 1 month.

Makes 10 cups

NOTE: The alcohol in the wine keeps the mixture from freezing rock hard. Thaw slightly before breaking up.

BELLINI SPLASH

½ cup V8 Splash® Mango Peach Juice Drink, chilled

¼ cup peach nectar, chilled

1 cup champagne, sparkling wine **or** sparkling cider, chilled

1. Stir the juice drink and nectar in a **1-cup** measure.

2. Divide the mixture between **2** fluted champagne glasses. Pour in the champagne.

3. Serve immediately.

Makes 2 servings

PREP TIME: 5 minutes
TOTAL TIME: 5 minutes

CARDAMOM-SPIKED FRESH LEMONADE SPRITZER

40 whole white cardamom
   pods, cracked

 3 cups water

1¼ cups sugar

 2 cups lemon juice

 1 bottle (750 ml) Asti
   Spumante or club soda

   Additional sugar (optional)

   Fresh mint leaves (optional)

1. Combine cardamom pods, water and 1¼ cups sugar in medium saucepan; bring to a boil over high heat, stirring until sugar dissolves. Reduce heat to low; cover and simmer 30 minutes. Remove from heat; cool completely. Refrigerate 2 hours or up to 3 days.

2. Pour mixture through strainer into 3-quart pitcher; discard pods. Stir in lemon juice and Asti Spumante. Add additional sugar to taste. Garnish with mint.

Makes 6 servings

MIMOSA

2 cups chilled orange juice

2 cups chilled champagne

Orange wedges or twists (optional)

Pour orange juice into champagne flutes; top with champagne. Garnish with orange wedges.

Makes 4 servings

CLASSIC BELLINI •

3 ounces peach nectar*

4 ounces chilled champagne or dry sparkling wine

Or peel and pit a ripe medium peach and purée in blender.

Pour peach nectar into chilled champagne flute; slowly pour in champagne. Stir gently.

Makes 1 serving

· ·

VIRGIN BELLINI

2 tablespoons peach nectar

¼ cup white grape juice

½ cup chilled sparkling cider

Combine peach nectar and grape juice in champagne flute; top with cider.

Makes 1 serving

CHAMPAGNE COCKTAIL •

1 sugar cube
   Dash of bitters
   Chilled champagne or
   dry sparkling wine

Place sugar cube in chilled champagne flute; sprinkle with bitters. Fill glass with champagne.

Makes 1 serving

CHAMPAGNE COOLER

1½ ounces brandy
 1 ounce triple sec
 1 cup chilled champagne

Combine brandy and triple sec in wine glass; top with champagne.

Makes 1 serving

TROPICAL CHAMPAGNE ICE

- 6 cups V8 Splash® Tropical Blend Juice Drink, chilled
- 1 bottle (750 mL) champagne **or** other sparkling wine, chilled
- 1 teaspoon grated orange zest (optional)
- 4½ cups cut-up fresh fruit (mango, papaya **or** pineapple)

1. Stir the juice drink, champagne and orange zest, if desired, in a 13×9×2-inch metal baking pan.

2. Cover the pan and freeze it for 3 hours, stirring with a fork every hour.

3. Scoop **about ½ cup** of the champagne ice into a stemmed glass or dessert glass. Top with the fruit. Serve immediately.

Makes 18 servings

PREP TIME: 15 minutes
FREEZE TIME: 3 hours
TOTAL TIME: 3 hours 15 minutes

KITCHEN TIP: If you have any leftover ice, wrap the pan with plastic wrap and store in the freezer. When you want to serve it, remove it from the freezer about 5 minutes before serving to allow it to soften a bit before scooping.

SPIRITED REFRESHERS

GINGER-CUCUMBER LIMEADE

1½ cups chopped seeded peeled cucumber

⅓ cup frozen limeade concentrate, thawed

1 teaspoon grated fresh ginger

1 cup chilled sparkling water

⅓ cup gin

Cucumber slices (optional)

Lime peel (optional)

1. Combine chopped cucumber, limeade concentrate and ginger in blender; blend until smooth.

2. Combine cucumber mixture, sparkling water and gin in small pitcher; stir gently. Serve immediately over ice. Garnish with cucumber slices and lime peel.

Makes 3 servings

CAMPARI COOLER

2 ounces orange juice

1 ounce Campari

1 ounce peach schnapps

Juice of 1 lime
(about 1½ tablespoons)

Club soda or lemon-lime
soda (optional)

Orange wedge and
maraschino cherry

Fill cocktail shaker half full with ice; add orange juice, Campari, peach schnapps and lime juice. Shake until blended; strain into ice-filled margarita or highball glass. Top with splash of club soda, if desired. Garnish with orange wedge and maraschino cherry.

Makes 1 serving

SALTY DOG ·

¾ cup grapefruit juice
   Salt
1½ ounces vodka

Moisten rim of martini glass with grapefruit juice; dip in salt. Fill glass with ice; pour vodka over ice. Stir in grapefruit juice.

Makes 1 serving

GREYHOUND: Omit salt.

PIMM'S CUP

2 ounces Pimm's No. 1
   Lemon-lime soda
   Cucumber strip or spear
   Lemon twist

Fill chilled highball glass with ice; pour in Pimm's. Fill with lemon-lime soda. Garnish with cucumber and lemon twist.

Makes 1 serving

ELECTRIC LEMONADE •

1½ ounces vodka

½ ounce blue curaçao

2 ounces sweet and sour mix

Lemon-lime soda

Lime wedges

Fill Collins glass half full with ice; add vodka, curaçao and sweet and sour mix. Fill with lemon-lime soda. Garnish with lime wedges.

Makes 1 serving

SUNLIGHT SIPPER

1½ cups DOLE® Pine-Orange Banana Juice, chilled

1 tablespoon peach schnapps

1 tablespoon light rum

1 tablespoon orange liqueur

Cracked ice

• **Pour** juice, schnapps, rum and liqueur into 2 glasses. Add ice. Garnish as desired.

Makes 2 servings

BLOODY MARY

Dash Worcestershire sauce, hot pepper sauce, celery salt, black pepper and salt

1½ ounces vodka

3 ounces tomato juice

½ ounce lemon juice

Celery stalk with leaves, pickle spear, lemon slice and/or green olives (optional)

Fill highball glass with ice; add dashes of Worcestershire sauce, hot pepper sauce, celery salt, black pepper and salt. Add vodka, tomato juice and lemon juice; stir gently. Serve with desired garnishes.

Makes 1 serving

BAY BREEZE •

1½ ounces vodka

½ cup pineapple juice

1 ounce cranberry juice

   Pineapple wedge

Fill highball glass or martini glass with ice; add vodka, pineapple juice and cranberry juice. Stir well. Garnish with pineapple wedge.

Makes 1 serving

FUZZY NAVEL

½ cup orange juice

1½ ounces peach schnapps

1 ounce vodka (optional)

   Orange slice

Fill cocktail shaker half full with ice; add orange juice, schnapps and vodka, if desired. Shake until blended; strain into chilled old fashioned glass or highball glass. Garnish with orange slice.

Makes 1 serving

PINEAPPLE MINT RUM JULEP

1 sprig fresh mint

   DOLE® Pineapple Juice cubes or ice, crushed

1 cup DOLE® Pineapple Juice *or* Pineapple Orange Juice

2 tablespoons powdered sugar

1½ ounces rum

   Additional mint sprig (optional)

• **Rub** mint sprig around inside of glass.

• **Partially** fill glass with crushed juice cubes. Pour in pineapple juice. Stir in powdered sugar and rum. Garnish with mint sprig, if desired.

Makes 1 serving

LONG ISLAND ICED TEA

½ ounce vodka

½ ounce tequila

½ ounce light rum

½ ounce gin

½ ounce triple sec

1 ounce lemon juice

1 teaspoon sugar or
simple syrup (see Tip)

Chilled cola

Lemon wedge and
maraschino cherry

Fill cocktail shaker half full with ice; add vodka, tequila, rum, gin, triple sec, lemon juice and sugar. Shake until blended; strain into ice-filled highball glass. Top with cola. Garnish with lemon wedge and maraschino cherry.

Makes 1 serving

TIP: To make simple syrup, bring 1 cup water to a boil; stir in 1 cup sugar. Cook over low heat until the sugar is dissolved, stirring constantly. Cool to room temperature. Store in a glass jar in the refrigerator.

SEA BREEZE

1½ ounces vodka

3 ounces cranberry juice

2 ounces grapefruit juice

Fill martini glass or highball glass with ice; add vodka, cranberry juice and grapefruit juice. Stir well.

Makes 1 serving

TOM COLLINS •

2 ounces gin

1 ounce lemon juice

1 teaspoon superfine sugar

3 ounces chilled club soda

Lemon slice

Fill cocktail shaker half full with ice; add gin, lemon juice and sugar. Shake until blended; strain into ice-filled Collins glass. Top with club soda. Garnish with lemon slice.

Makes 1 serving

. . . .

NEGRONI

1 ounce gin

1 ounce Campari

1 ounce sweet or dry vermouth

Lemon twist

Fill cocktail shaker half full with ice; add gin, Campari and vermouth. Shake until blended; strain into chilled cocktail glass. Garnish with lemon twist.

Makes 1 serving

LIME RICKEY

- 2 ounces vodka
- 2 ounces gin
- 2 ounces lime juice
- Club soda
- Lime wedge
- Fresh mint leaves

Fill cocktail glass with ice; add vodka, gin and lime juice. Fill with club soda. Garnish with lime wedge and mint.

Makes 1 serving

RASPBERRY RICKEY: Place ⅓ cup fresh raspberries in small bowl; sprinkle with 2 teaspoons sugar. Add 2 ounces lime juice; let stand 10 minutes. Press through sieve to remove seeds. Combine raspberry mixture, 2 ounces raspberry-flavored vodka and 2 ounces gin in ice-filled old fashioned glass. Fill with club soda. Garnish with additional raspberries and fresh mint leaves.

PITCHERS & PUNCHES

STRAWBERRY-APRICOT PUNCH

- 2 packages (10 ounces each) frozen sliced strawberries in syrup, thawed
- 2 cans (5½ ounces each) apricot or peach nectar
- ¼ cup lemon juice
- 2 tablespoons honey
- 2 bottles (750 ml each) chilled champagne or sparkling wine

  Lemon slices and fresh strawberry halves

1. Place strawberries with syrup in food processor or blender; process until smooth.

2. Pour puréed strawberries into large punch bowl. Stir in apricot nectar, lemon juice and honey until well blended.

3. Just before serving, stir champagne into strawberry mixture. Garnish with lemon slices and fresh strawberry halves.

Makes 12 servings

BUBBLING RASPBERRY COOLERS

¾ cup raspberry vinegar

½ cup sugar

2 liters seltzer water

2 cups fresh raspberries

Fresh mint leaves

1. Combine vinegar and sugar in small saucepan; bring to a boil over medium heat. Boil 1 minute or until sugar is dissolved, stirring frequently. Set aside to cool.

2. Pour cooled syrup into large pitcher; stir in seltzer water. To serve, fill each glass with ice, ¼ cup raspberries and mint leaves. Fill glasses with selzer mixture. Serve immediately.

Makes 8 to 10 servings

CITRUS COOLER

- 2 cups orange juice
- 2 cups pineapple juice
- 1 teaspoon lemon juice
- ¾ teaspoon coconut extract
- ¾ teaspoon vanilla
- 2 cups chilled sparkling wine

1. Combine orange juice, pineapple juice, lemon juice, coconut extract and vanilla in large pitcher; refrigerate until cold.

2. Just before serving, stir in sparkling wine. Serve over ice.

Makes 9 servings

PINEAPPLE-LEMONADE PIZZAZZ

3 cups chilled peach nectar, mango nectar or peach-mango juice

3 cups chilled pineapple juice

1 can (12 ounces) frozen lemonade concentrate, thawed

2½ cups chilled club soda or sparkling water

2 cups chilled ginger ale

1½ cups vodka

1. Combine peach nectar, pineapple juice and lemonade concentrate in large pitcher.

2. Gently stir in club soda, ginger ale and vodka. Serve immediately over crushed ice.

Makes 12 servings

CUCUMBER PUNCH

1 English cucumber,
   thinly sliced

1 cup water

½ (12-ounce) can thawed
   frozen limeade concentrate

1 bottle (1 liter) chilled club
   soda

1 cup light rum or vodka

   Lime wedges

1. Combine cucumber, water
and limeade concentrate in
punch bowl or large pitcher.
Refrigerate 1 hour.

2. Just before serving, stir in
club soda and rum. Pour into
ice-filled glasses. Garnish with
lime wedges.

Makes 10 servings

SUPER FRUITY CITRUS PUNCH

- 4 oranges, sectioned
- 1 pint fresh strawberries, stemmed and halved
- 1 to 2 limes, cut into 1/8-inch slices
- 1 lemon, cut into 1/8-inch slices
- 1 cup fresh raspberries
- 2 cups orange juice
- 2 cups grapefruit juice
- 3/4 cup lime juice
- 1/2 cup light corn syrup
- 1 bottle (750 ml) Asti Spumante, sparkling wine, ginger ale or white grape juice
- Fresh mint leaves

1. Spread orange sections, strawberries, lime slices, lemon slices and raspberries on baking sheet. Freeze 4 hours or until firm.

2. Combine juices and corn syrup in large pitcher; stir until corn syrup dissolves. Refrigerate 2 hours or until cold. Just before serving, stir in Asti Spumanti.

3. Divide frozen fruit among large (12-ounce) glasses. Fill glasses with punch. Garnish with mint.

Makes 8 to 10 servings

CRANBERRY-PINEAPPLE PUNCH

2½ cups chilled cranberry juice

2 cups chilled pineapple juice

2½ cups chilled champagne

Combine cranberry juice and pineapple juice in large pitcher. Gently stir in champagne. Serve over ice.

Makes about 8 servings

CHAMPAGNE PUNCH

1 orange

1 lemon

¼ cup cranberry-flavored liqueur or cognac

¼ cup orange-flavored liqueur or triple sec

1 bottle (750 ml) chilled sparkling pink or white wine or champagne

Fresh cranberries (optional)

1. Remove colored peel, not white pith, from orange and lemon in long thin strips using citrus peeler. Refrigerate orange and lemon for another use. Combine peels and liqueurs in medium pitcher. Refrigerate 2 to 6 hours.

2. Just before serving, tilt pitcher to one side and slowly pour in sparkling wine. (Leave peels in pitcher for added flavor.) Place cranberries in bottom of each champagne glass, if desired; fill glasses with punch.

Makes 6 to 8 servings

STRAWBERRY-PEACH COOLER

1 cup sliced fresh strawberries

1 cup chopped fresh peaches

2 tablespoons sugar

1 bottle (750 ml) chilled white wine

1 bottle (1 quart) chilled sparkling water

Fresh mint leaves

1. Combine strawberries and peaches in small bowl. Sprinkle with sugar; stir gently. Let stand at room temperature 30 minutes.

2. Pour fruit into punch bowl. Gently stir in wine and sparkling water. Serve over ice. Garnish with mint.

Makes about 2 quarts

NONALCOHOLIC STRAWBERRY-PEACH COOLER: Reduce sugar to 1 tablespoon and substitute 1 quart apple juice for the wine.

FESTIVE CITRUS PUNCH

1 can (6 ounces) frozen Florida grapefruit juice concentrate, thawed

1 can (6 ounces) frozen pineapple juice concentrate, thawed

1 cup water

3 tablespoons honey

2 tablespoons grenadine syrup (optional)

1 bottle (1 liter) ginger ale, chilled

Mint sprigs for garnish (optional)

Combine grapefruit juice concentrate, pineapple juice concentrate, water and honey in punch bowl or large pitcher. Stir in grenadine, if desired. Stir until well combined.

Just before serving, slowly pour ginger ale down side of punch bowl. Stir gently to combine. Garnish, if desired. Serve over ice in chilled glasses.

Makes about 18 (4-ounce) servings

*Favorite recipe from **Florida Department of Citrus***

ONE-BITE WONDERS

CREAMY MUSHROOM CUPS

- 2 tablespoons butter
- 4 ounces mushrooms, coarsely chopped
- ¼ teaspoon salt
- 2 cloves garlic, minced
- 2 tablespoons dry sherry
- ¼ cup whipping cream
- 15 frozen mini phyllo shells, thawed and heated according to package directions
- ¼ cup chopped fresh parsley

1. Melt butter in large nonstick skillet over medium heat. Add mushrooms and salt; cook and stir 5 minutes or until tender. Add garlic; cook and stir 15 seconds.

2. Stir in sherry until well blended. Add cream; cook and stir 2 minutes or until thickened.

3. Spoon mushroom mixture into phyllo shells; sprinkle with parsley. Serve immediately.

Makes 5 servings

41

BRANDY-SOAKED SCALLOPS

1 pound bacon, cut in half crosswise

2 pounds small sea scallops

½ cup brandy

⅓ cup olive oil

2 tablespoons chopped fresh parsley

1 clove garlic, minced

1 teaspoon black pepper

½ teaspoon salt

½ teaspoon onion powder

1. Wrap one piece bacon around each scallop; secure with toothpick, if necessary. Place wrapped scallops in 13×9-inch baking dish.

2. Combine brandy, oil, parsley, garlic, pepper, salt and onion powder in small bowl; mix well. Pour mixture over scallops; cover and marinate in refrigerator at least 4 hours.

3. Preheat broiler. Remove scallops from marinade; discard marinade. Arrange scallops on rack of broiler pan.

4. Broil 4 inches from heat 7 to 10 minutes or until bacon is browned. Turn and broil 5 minutes or until scallops are opaque.

Makes 8 servings

MINI EGG ROLLS

8 ounces ground pork

3 cloves garlic, minced

1 teaspoon minced fresh ginger

¼ teaspoon red pepper flakes

6 cups (12 ounces) shredded coleslaw mix

¼ cup reduced-sodium soy sauce

1 tablespoon cornstarch

1 tablespoon seasoned rice vinegar

½ cup chopped green onions

28 wonton wrappers

Peanut or canola oil for frying

Prepared sweet and sour sauce

Chinese hot mustard

1. Combine pork, garlic, ginger and red pepper flakes in large nonstick skillet; cook and stir over medium heat about 4 minutes or until pork is cooked through, stirring to break up meat. Add coleslaw mix; cover and cook 2 minutes. Uncover and cook 2 minutes or until coleslaw mix just begins to wilt.

2. Whisk soy sauce and cornstarch in small bowl until smooth and well blended; stir into pork mixture. Add vinegar; cook 2 to 3 minutes or until sauce is thickened. Remove from heat; stir in green onions.

3. Working with one wonton wrapper at a time, place wrapper on clean work surface. Spoon 1 level tablespoon pork mixture across and just below center of wrapper. Fold bottom point of wrapper up over filling; fold side points over filling, forming envelope shape. Moisten inside edges of top point with water and roll egg roll toward top point, pressing firmly to seal. Repeat with remaining wrappers and filling.

4. Heat ¼ inch of oil in large skillet over medium heat. Fry egg rolls in small batches 2 minutes per side or until golden brown. Remove with splotted spoon to paper towel-lined plate. Serve immediately with sweet and sour sauce and mustard for dipping.

Makes 28 mini egg rolls

ELEGANT SHRIMP SCAMPI

¼ cup (½ stick) plus
  2 tablespoons butter

6 to 8 cloves garlic, minced

1½ pounds large raw shrimp
  (about 16), peeled and
  deveined (with tails on)

6 green onions, thinly sliced

¼ cup dry white wine

  Juice of 1 lemon
  (about 2 tablespoons)

¼ cup chopped fresh parsley

  Salt and black pepper

  Lemon slices (optional)

1. Clarify butter by melting it in small saucepan over low heat. *Do not stir.* Skim off white foam that forms on top. Strain clarified butter through a cheesecloth into glass measuring cup to yield ⅓ cup. Discard cheesecloth and milky residue at bottom of pan.

2. Heat clarified butter in large skillet over medium heat. Add garlic; cook and stir 1 to 2 minutes or until softened but not browned.

3. Add shrimp, green onions, wine and lemon juice. Cook and stir 3 to 4 minutes or until shrimp are pink and opaque. *Do not overcook.*

4. Stir in parsley; season with salt and pepper. Garnish with lemon slices.

Makes 8 servings

GLAZED BACON-WRAPPED DATES

8 slices bacon, cut in half crosswise

⅓ cup cola

2 tablespoons balsamic vinegar

1 teaspoon Dijon mustard

⅛ teaspoon garlic powder

16 large dates

8 teaspoons cream cheese, divided

16 raw, roasted or smoked almonds

1 tablespoon butter

½ teaspoon salt

½ teaspoon black pepper

1. Preheat oven to 400°F. Cook bacon in medium skillet over medium heat 1 minute per side. (Bacon should be soft.) Drain on paper towel-lined plate. Drain off drippings.

2. Add cola, vinegar, mustard and garlic powder to skillet; cook 3 to 4 minutes or until mixture thickens, stirring occasionally.

3. Cut lengthwise slit down one side of each date and remove pit. Fill each date with ½ teaspoon cream cheese and 1 almond; pinch date closed.

4. Wrap each stuffed date with ½ slice bacon; secure with wooden toothpick. Remove glaze from heat; stir in butter, salt and pepper. Roll dates in glaze to coat; arrange on nonstick rimmed baking sheets. Drizzle any remaining glaze over dates.

5. Bake 10 minutes. Let stand 5 minutes before serving.

Makes 8 servings

FRENCH-STYLE PIZZA BITES

2 tablespoons olive oil

1 medium onion, thinly sliced

1 medium red bell pepper, cut into 3-inch strips

2 cloves garlic, minced

⅓ cup pitted black olives, cut into thin wedges

1 package (about 14 ounces ounces) refrigerated pizza dough

¾ cup (3 ounces) finely shredded Swiss or Gruyère cheese

1. Place oven rack in lowest position. Preheat oven to 425°F. Line large baking sheet with parchment paper or spray with nonstick cooking spray.

2. Heat oil in medium skillet over medium heat. Add onion, bell pepper and garlic; cook and stir 5 minutes or until crisp-tender. Stir in olives. Remove from heat.

3. Pat dough into 16×12-inch rectangle on prepared baking sheet. Arrange onion mixture over dough; sprinkle with cheese.

4. Bake 10 minutes. Loosen crust with long spatula; slide directly onto oven rack. Bake 3 to 5 minutes or until golden brown.

5. Slide baking sheet under crust to remove pizza from oven; transfer to cutting board. Cut pizza crosswise into eight 1¾-inch-wide strips, then cut diagonally into ten 2-inch-wide strips to create diamond pieces. Serve immediately.

Makes about 24 pieces

TURKEY MEATBALLS WITH YOGURT-CUCUMBER SAUCE

2 tablespoons olive oil, divided

1 cup finely chopped onion

2 cloves garlic, minced

1¼ pounds ground turkey
  or ground lamb

½ cup plain dry bread crumbs

¼ cup whipping cream

1 egg, lightly beaten

3 tablespoons chopped
  fresh mint

1 teaspoon salt

⅛ teaspoon ground red pepper

  Yogurt-Cucumber Sauce
  (recipe follows)

1. Line two baking sheets with parchment paper. Heat 1 tablespoon oil in medium skillet over medium-high heat. Add onion; cook and stir 3 minutes or until softened. Add garlic; cook and stir 30 seconds. Let cool slightly.

2. Combine turkey, onion mixture, bread crumbs, cream, egg, mint, salt and red pepper in large bowl; mix gently. Shape mixture into 40 meatballs. Place meatballs on prepared baking sheets. Cover with plastic wrap; refrigerate 1 hour.

3. Meanwhile, prepare Yogurt-Cucumber Sauce. Preheat oven to 400°F. Brush meatballs with remaining 1 tablespoon oil.

4. Bake 15 to 20 minutes or until cooked through, turning once during baking. Serve with sauce.

Makes 40 meatballs

YOGURT-CUCUMBER SAUCE

1 container (6 ounces) plain Greek yogurt

½ cup peeled seeded and finely chopped
  cucumber

2 teaspoons chopped fresh mint

2 teaspoons grated lemon peel

2 teaspoons lemon juice

¼ teaspoon salt

Combine all ingredients in small bowl; mix well. Refrigerate until ready to serve.

Makes about 1 cup

CHICKPEA CAKES

1 can (about 15 ounces) chickpeas, rinsed and drained

1 cup shredded carrots

⅓ cup seasoned dry bread crumbs

¼ cup creamy Italian salad dressing, plus additional for dipping

1 egg

1. Preheat oven to 375°F. Spray baking sheets with nonstick cooking spray.

2. Coarsely mash chickpeas in medium bowl with potato masher. Stir in carrots, bread crumbs, ¼ cup salad dressing and egg; mix well.

3. Shape mixture into 24 patties, using about 1 tablespoon for each. Place on prepared baking sheets.

4. Bake 15 to 18 minutes or until lightly browned on both sides, turning halfway through baking time. Serve warm with additional salad dressing for dipping.

Makes about 24 cakes

SWEET AND SPICY SAUSAGE ROUNDS

1 pound kielbasa sausage, cut into ¼-inch-thick rounds

⅔ cup blackberry jam

⅓ cup steak sauce

1 tablespoon yellow mustard

½ teaspoon ground allspice

Slow Cooker Directions

1. Combine sausage, jam, steak sauce, mustard and allspice in slow cooker; mix well.

2. Cover; cook on HIGH 3 hours. Serve with decorative cocktail picks.

Makes about 16 servings

MINI ASPARAGUS QUICHES

8 stalks asparagus, trimmed
3 eggs
¼ teaspoon salt
¼ teaspoon black pepper
1 unbaked 9-inch pie crust

1. Preheat oven to 300°F. Spray 20 mini (1¾-inch) muffin cups with nonstick cooking spray.

2. Cut asparagus diagonally into thin slices or coarsely chop enough to make ½ cup. Bring 3 cups water to a boil in medium saucepan over medium heat. Add asparagus; cook 2 minutes. Drain and rinse under cold water.

3. Whisk eggs, salt and pepper in medium bowl until blended. Stir in asparagus.

4. Roll out pie crust into 13-inch circle. Cut out circles with 3-inch round biscuit cutter. Gather and reroll scraps to make 20 circles total. Press circles into prepared muffin cups. Fill with egg mixture.

5. Bake 30 minutes or until tops are lightly browned and toothpick inserted into centers comes out clean.

Makes 20 mini quiches

MINI SWISS QUICHES: Prepare dough circles as directed. Whisk 4 eggs, ¼ teaspoon salt and ¼ teaspoon black pepper until blended; stir in ¾ cup shredded Swiss cheese. Fill cups with egg mixture. Bake as directed. Makes 20 mini quiches.

CRAB-STUFFED TOMATOES

16 large cherry tomatoes
    (1½ inches in diameter)

3 tablespoons mayonnaise

½ teaspoon lemon juice

1 small clove garlic, minced

¾ cup fresh or refrigerated
    canned crabmeat*

3 tablespoons chopped
    pimiento-stuffed
    green olives

2 tablespoons slivered almonds
    or pine nuts

⅛ teaspoon black pepper

Choose special grade crabmeat for this recipe. It is less expensive and already flaked but just as flavorful as backfin, lump or claw meat. Look for it in the refrigerated seafood section of the supermarket. Shelf-stable canned crabmeat can be substituted..

1. Cut small slivers from bottoms of cherry tomatoes so they will stand upright. Cut off tops of tomatoes; scoop out seeds and membranes. Turn tomatoes upside down to drain.

2. Combine mayonnaise, lemon juice and garlic in medium bowl. Add crabmeat, olives, almonds and pepper; mix well.

3. Spoon crab mixture into tomatoes. Serve immediately.

Makes 8 to 10 servings

NOTE: If large cherry tomatoes are unavailable, you can substitute 4 small plum tomatoes. Cut tomatoes in half lengthwise; scoop out seeds and membranes. Turn cut sides down to drain; set aside. Proceed as directed above.

TIP: For the best flavor, do not refrigerate the stuffed tomatoes. The crab mixture can be prepared several hours in advance and refrigerated. Stuff the tomatoes just before serving. Or, serve the crab mixture on crackers or toasted French bread rounds.

MICRO MINI STUFFED POTATOES

1 pound small new red potatoes

¼ cup sour cream

2 tablespoons butter, softened

½ teaspoon minced garlic

¼ cup milk

½ cup (2 ounces) shredded sharp Cheddar cheese

½ teaspoon salt

¼ teaspoon black pepper

¼ cup finely chopped green onions (optional)

1. Pierce potatoes with fork in several places. Microwave potatoes on HIGH 5 to 6 minutes or until tender. Let stand 5 minutes. Cut potatoes in half lengthwise; scoop out pulp. Set potato shells aside.

2. Beat potato pulp in medium bowl with electric mixer at low speed 30 seconds. Add sour cream, butter and garlic; beat until well blended. Gradually add milk; beat until smooth. Add Cheddar, salt and pepper; beat until well blended. Spoon into potato shells.

3. Microwave on HIGH 1 to 2 minutes or until cheese melts. Garnish with green onions.

Makes 4 servings

SPICY POLENTA CHEESE BITES

3 cups water
1 cup corn grits or cornmeal
½ teaspoon salt
¼ teaspoon chili powder
1 tablespoon butter
¼ cup minced onion or shallot
1 tablespoon minced jalapeño
  pepper*
½ cup (2 ounces) shredded
  sharp Cheddar or
  fontina cheese

Jalapeño peppers can sting and irritate the skin, so wear rubber gloves when handling peppers and do not touch your eyes.

1. Spray 8-inch square baking pan with nonstick cooking spray. Bring water to a boil in large nonstick saucepan over high heat. Gradually add grits, stirring constantly. Reduce heat to low; cook and stir until grits are tender and water is absorbed. Stir in salt and chili powder. Remove from heat.

2. Melt butter in small saucepan over medium-high heat. Add onion and jalapeño; cook and stir 3 to 5 minutes or until tender. Stir into grits; mix well. Spread mixture in prepared pan. Let stand 1 hour or until cool and firm.

3. Preheat broiler. Cut polenta into 16 squares. Arrange squares on nonstick baking sheet; sprinkle with Cheddar.

4. Broil 4 inches from heat source 5 minutes or until cheese is melted and slightly browned. Cut squares in half. Serve warm or at room temperature.

Makes 32 appetizers

TIP: For spicier flavor, add ⅛ teaspoon red pepper flakes to the onion mixture.

QUICK CRISPY RANCH CHICKEN BITES

¾ cup ranch dressing, plus additional for serving

2 cups panko bread crumbs

1 pound boneless skinless chicken breasts, cut into 1-inch pieces

1. Preheat oven to 375°F. Line baking sheet with foil; spray foil with nonstick cooking spray.

2. Place ¾ cup ranch dressing in shallow bowl. Spread panko in another shallow bowl. Dip chicken in dressing; shake off excess. Roll in panko to coat. Place breaded chicken on prepared baking sheet; spray with cooking spray.

3. Bake 15 to 17 minutes or until golden brown and cooked through, turning once. Serve with additional ranch dressing.

Makes 4 servings

BACON-WRAPPED APRICOTS

14 slices bacon, cut in half crosswise

¼ cup packed brown sugar

½ teaspoon black pepper

28 Mediterranean dried apricots* (one 7-ounce package)

14 water chestnuts, drained and cut in half crosswise

Mediterranean dried apricots are plump, pitted whole apricots, available in the dried fruit section of most supermarkets.

1. Preheat oven to 425°F. Line shallow baking pan or baking sheet with parchment paper.

2. Sprinkle bacon with brown sugar and pepper, pressing to adhere. Fold apricot around water chestnut half. Wrap with half slice bacon; secure with toothpick.

3. Arrange apricots in prepared pan, spacing at least 1 inch apart. Bake about 20 minutes or until bacon is cooked through, turning once.

Makes 14 servings

BARBECUED MEATBALLS

2 pounds ground beef

1⅓ cups ketchup, divided

1 egg, lightly beaten

3 tablespoons seasoned dry bread crumbs

2 tablespoons dried onion flakes

¾ teaspoon garlic salt

½ teaspoon black pepper

1 cup packed brown sugar

1 can (6 ounces) tomato paste

¼ cup reduced-sodium soy sauce

¼ cup cider vinegar

1½ teaspoons hot pepper sauce

Chopped bell peppers (optional)

Slow Cooker Directions

1. Preheat oven to 350°F. Combine beef, ⅓ cup ketchup, egg, bread crumbs, onion flakes, garlic salt and black pepper in large bowl; mix gently. Shape mixture into 1-inch meatballs. Arrange in single layer on two 15×10-inch jelly-roll pans.

2. Bake 18 minutes or until browned. Transfer meatballs to slow cooker.

3. Combine remaining 1 cup ketchup, brown sugar, tomato paste, soy sauce, vinegar and hot pepper sauce in medium bowl; mix well. Pour over meatballs.

4. Cover; cook on LOW 4 hours. Serve with cocktail picks. Garnish with bell peppers, if desired.

Makes about 48 meatballs

BARBECUED FRANKS: Place two (12-ounce) packages or three (8-ounce) packages cocktail franks in slow cooker. Prepare ketchup mixture as directed in step 3; pour over franks. Cover; cook on LOW 4 hours.

SAUSAGE AND FENNEL STUFFED MUSHROOMS

18 large brown mushrooms
   (about 2 inches diameter)

2 teaspoons olive oil

¾ cup finely chopped fennel
   (3 to 4 ounces),
   tops reserved

2 cloves garlic, minced

½ teaspoon dried thyme

¼ teaspoon coarse salt

½ teaspoon black pepper

1 package (12 ounces) fully
   cooked smoked apple
   chicken sausage links,
   finely chopped

4 ounces cream cheese,
   softened

½ cup grated Parmesan
   cheese, divided

4 tablespoons Italian-style
   dry bread crumbs, divided

1 cup chicken broth

   Fresh fennel fronds
   (optional)

1. Preheat oven to 375°F. Clean mushrooms with damp paper towels. Remove and chop stems.

2. Heat oil in medium skillet over medium heat. Add chopped fennel; cook and stir 3 minutes or until softened. Add garlic, thyme, salt and pepper; cook and stir 1 minute. Add sausage and mushroom stems; cook 6 to 8 minutes or until sausage is lightly browned, stirring occasionally. Remove from heat.

3. Chop reserved fennel tops. Add cream cheese, ¼ cup Parmesan, 2 tablespoons bread crumbs and 1 tablespoon finely chopped fennel tops to sausage mixture; mix well. (Discard remaining chopped fennel tops or save for another use.)

4. Spray mushroom caps with nonstick cooking spray. Sprinkle lightly with additional salt and pepper. Fill each cap with about 1 tablespoon sausage mixure; place in 15×10-inch jelly-roll pan or two 13×9-inch baking dishes. Pour broth around mushrooms; sprinkle with remaining ¼ cup Parmesan and 2 tablespoons bread crumbs.

5. Bake 20 to 25 minutes or until mushrooms are golden brown. Let stand 5 minutes before serving. Garnish with fennel fronds, if desired.

Makes 6 servings

BREADS & SPREADS

MEDITERRANEAN PITA PIZZAS

2 (8-inch) pita bread rounds

1 teaspoon olive oil

1 cup canned cannellini beans, rinsed and drained

2 teaspoons lemon juice

2 cloves garlic, minced

½ cup thinly sliced radicchio or escarole lettuce (optional)

½ cup chopped seeded tomato

½ cup finely chopped red onion

¼ cup (1 ounce) crumbled feta cheese

2 tablespoons sliced pitted black olives

1. Preheat oven to 450°F. Arrange pitas on baking sheet; brush with oil. Bake 6 minutes.

2. Meanwhile, place beans in small bowl; mash lightly with fork. Stir in lemon juice and garlic.

3. Spread bean mixture on pitas to within ½ inch of edges. Top with radicchio, if desired, tomato, onion, feta and olives. Bake 5 minutes or until toppings are heated through and crust is crisp. Cut into wedges; serve warm.

Makes 4 servings

FOCACCIA

1 package (¼ ounce)
   active dry yeast

1 teaspoon sugar

1½ cups warm water
   (105° to 110°F)

4 cups all-purpose flour,
   divided

7 tablespoons olive oil, divided

1 teaspoon salt

¼ cup bottled roasted red
   peppers, drained and
   cut into strips

¼ cup pitted black olives

1. Stir yeast and sugar into warm water in large bowl until dissolved. Let stand 5 minutes or until bubbly. Add 3½ cups flour, 3 tablespoons oil and salt; stir until soft dough forms.

2. Turn out dough onto lightly floured surface. Knead 5 minutes or until smooth and elastic, gradually adding remaining flour to prevent sticking, if necessary. Shape dough into a ball. Place in large greased bowl; turn to grease top. Cover and let rise in warm place 1 hour or until doubled in size.

3. Brush 15×10-inch jelly-roll pan with 1 tablespoon oil. Punch down dough. Turn out dough onto lightly floured surface. Flatten into rectangle; roll out almost to size of pan. Place dough in pan; gently press dough to edges. Poke surface of dough with end of wooden spoon handle, making indentations every 1 or 2 inches.

4. Brush dough with remaining 3 tablespoons oil; gently press roasted peppers and olives into dough. Cover and let rise in warm place 30 minutes or until doubled in size. Preheat oven to 450°F.

5. Bake 12 to 18 minutes or until golden brown. Cut into squares or rectangles. Serve warm.

Makes 12 servings

ONION AND WHITE BEAN SPREAD

1 can (about 15 ounces) cannellini or Great Northern beans, rinsed and drained

¼ cup chopped green onions

¼ cup grated Parmesan cheese

¼ cup olive oil, plus additional for drizzling

1 tablespoon fresh rosemary, chopped

2 cloves garlic, minced

French bread slices

1. Combine beans, green onions, Parmesan, ¼ cup oil, rosemary and garlic in food processor; process 30 to 40 seconds or until almost smooth.

2. Spoon bean mixture into serving bowl. Drizzle additional oil over spread just before serving. Serve with bread.

Makes 1¼ cups

TIP: For a more rustic-looking spread, place all ingredients in a medium bowl and mash with a potato masher.

SMOKY BACON MUSHROOM TOASTS

10 slices bacon

1 onion, diced

1 red bell pepper, diced

2 packages (8 ounces each)
   mushrooms, diced

   Salt and black pepper

24 (½-inch) toasted French
   bread slices

   Chopped fresh parsley

1. Cook bacon in large skillet over medium heat until crisp. Remove to paper towel-lined plate. Drain all but 2 tablespoons drippings from skillet.

2. Add onion and bell pepper to skillet; cook and stir over medium-high heat 2 minutes or until tender. Add mushrooms; season with salt and black pepper. Cook and stir 8 to 10 minutes or until liquid is evaporated. Cool 5 minutes.

3. Crumble bacon. Spread mushroom mixture on bread slices; sprinkle with bacon and parsley.

Makes 24 appetizers

RUSTIC VEGETABLE PIZZA

1 (10-ounce) prepared
  whole wheat pizza crust

2 large plum tomatoes,
  thinly sliced

1 tablespoon olive oil

2 small zucchini, thinly sliced

1 small eggplant, peeled
  and thinly sliced

⅓ cup sliced red onion

¼ teaspoon garlic salt

¾ cup (3 ounces) shredded
  mozzarella cheese

2 tablespoons grated
  Romano cheese

3 tablespoons chopped
  fresh basil

1. Preheat oven to 450°F. Place pizza crust on baking sheet. Arrange tomatoes on crust.

2. Heat oil in large skillet over medium-high heat. Add zucchini, eggplant, onion and garlic salt; cook and stir 4 to 5 minutes or until vegetables are crisp-tender. Layer vegetables over tomatoes on crust; sprinkle with mozzarella and Romano.

3. Bake 10 to 12 minutes or until cheeses are melted and crust is golden brown. Sprinkle with basil.

Makes 6 servings

EGGPLANT APPETIZER

1 medium eggplant
  (about 1 pound)

¼ pound ground beef

¼ cup finely chopped onion

1 clove garlic, minced

1 large tomato, chopped

1 small green bell pepper,
  finely chopped

¼ cup diced pimiento-stuffed
  green olives

2 tablespoons olive oil

1 tablespoon chopped fresh
  oregano *or* 1 teaspoon
  dried oregano

1 teaspoon white wine vinegar

Salt and black pepper

Toasted split mini pita bread
  rounds or baguette slices

1. Preheat oven to 350°F. Pierce eggplant several times with fork; place in shallow baking pan. Bake 1 hour or until skin is wrinkled and eggplant is soft. Set aside until cool enough to handle.

2. Meanwhile, brown beef in medium skillet over medium heat, stirring to break up meat. Drain fat. Add onion and garlic; cook and stir until tender.

3. Peel eggplant; cut into small cubes. Combine eggplant, ground beef mixture, tomato, bell pepper and olives in medium bowl.

4. Combine oil, oregano and vinegar in small bowl; mix well. Add to eggplant mixture; mix gently. Season with salt and black pepper. Serve on pitas.

Makes about 8 servings

ONION AND SHRIMP FLATBREAD BITES

4 teaspoons olive oil, divided

3 large onions, thinly sliced

¼ teaspoon salt

1 package (about 14 ounces) refrigerated pizza dough

½ pound small shrimp, peeled

⅛ cup chopped fresh chives

3 ounces goat cheese, crumbled

½ teaspoon black pepper

1. Heat 2 teaspoons oil in large skillet over medium heat. Add onions; cook and stir 8 minutes. Stir in salt. Reduce heat to medium-low; cook 25 minutes or until onions are deep golden brown, stirring occasionally.

2. Meanwhile, preheat oven to 425°F. Roll out dough on 15×10-inch jelly-roll pan. Bake 8 to 10 minutes or until crust is golden brown. Turn off oven. Spread caramelized onions over crust.

3. Heat remaining 2 teaspoons oil in same skillet over medium heat. Add shrimp; cook and stir 2 minutes or until pink and opaque. Arrange shrimp over onions on crust; sprinkle with chives, goat cheese and pepper.

4. Place flatbread in warm oven 1 to 2 minutes or until cheese is soft. Cut into 12 squares.

Makes 6 servings

BEANS AND GREENS CROSTINI

4 tablespoons olive oil, divided

1 small onion, thinly sliced

4 cups thinly sliced Italian black kale or other dinosaur kale variety

2 tablespoons minced garlic, divided

1 tablespoon balsamic vinegar

2 teaspoons salt, divided

¼ teaspoon red pepper flakes

1 can (about 15 ounces) cannellini beans, rinsed and drained

1 tablespoon chopped fresh rosemary

Toasted baguette slices

1. Heat 1 tablespoon oil in large skillet over medium heat. Add onion; cook and stir 5 minutes or until softened. Add kale and 1 tablespoon garlic; cook 15 minutes or until kale is softened and most of liquid has evaporated, stirring occasionally. Stir in vinegar, 1 teaspoon salt and red pepper flakes.

2. Meanwhile, combine beans, remaining 3 tablespoons oil, 1 tablespoon garlic, 1 teaspoon salt and rosemary in food processor; process until smooth.

3. Spread bean mixture on baguette slices; top with kale.

Makes about 24 crostini

BALSAMIC ONION AND PROSCIUTTO PIZZETTES

1 pound refrigerated pizza dough*

2 tablespoons extra virgin olive oil, divided

1 large or 2 small red onions, cut in half and thinly sliced

¼ teaspoon salt

1½ tablespoons balsamic vinegar

⅛ teaspoon black pepper

⅔ cup grated Parmesan cheese

4 ounces fresh mozzarella, cut into small pieces

1 package (about 3 ounces) thinly sliced prosciutto, cut or torn into small pieces

Refrigerated pizza dough can be found in 1-pound packages in the prepared foods section of many supermarkets. Frozen pizza dough can also be used; thaw according to package directions.

1. Remove dough from refrigerator; let rest at room temperature while preparing onions. Heat 1 tablespoon oil in medium skillet over medium-high heat. Add onion and salt; cook about 20 minutes or until tender and golden brown, stirring occasionally. Add vinegar and pepper; cook and stir 2 minutes. Set aside to cool.

2. Preheat oven to 450°F. Line two baking sheets with parchment paper.

3. Divide dough into 16 balls; press into 3-inch rounds (about ⅜ inch thick) on prepared baking sheets. Brush rounds with remaining 1 tablespoon oil; sprinkle with about 1 teaspoon Parmesan. Top with onion mixture, mozzarella, prosciutto and remaining Parmesan.

4. Bake about 13 minutes or until crusts are golden brown.

Makes 16 pizzettes

LAVASH CHIPS WITH ARTICHOKE PESTO

3 pieces lavash bread (7½×9½ inches)

¼ cup plus 2 tablespoons olive oil, divided

¾ teaspoon coarse salt, divided

1 can (14 ounces) artichoke hearts, rinsed and drained

½ cup chopped walnuts, toasted*

¼ cup packed fresh basil leaves

1 clove garlic, minced

2 tablespoons lemon juice

¼ cup grated Parmesan cheese

To toast walnuts, spread on baking sheet. Bake in preheated 350°F oven 6 to 8 minutes or until golden brown, stirring frequently. Immediately remove from pan; cool before using.

1. Preheat oven to 350°F. Line two baking sheets with parchment paper. Position oven racks in upper third and lower third of oven.

2. Brush both sides of each piece of lavash with 2 tablespoons oil; sprinkle with ¼ teaspoon salt. Bake 10 minutes or until lavash is crisp and browned, rotating baking sheets from front to back and top to bottom after 5 minutes. Remove to wire racks to cool completely.

3. Combine artichokes, walnuts, basil, garlic, lemon juice and remaining ½ teaspoon salt in food processor; pulse about 12 times or until coarsely chopped. With motor running, slowly add remaining ¼ cup oil until smooth. Add Parmesan; pulse just until blended.

4. Break lavash into chips. Serve with pesto.

Makes 6 servings (about 1½ cups pesto)

RED PEPPER ANTIPASTO

1 tablespoon olive oil

3 red bell peppers, cut into 2×¼-inch strips

2 cloves garlic, minced

2 tablespoons red wine vinegar

¼ teaspoon salt

Black pepper

1. Heat oil in large skillet over medium-high heat. Add bell peppers; cook and stir 8 to 9 minutes or until edges of peppers begin to brown. Reduce heat to medium. Add garlic; cook and stir 1 minute.

2. Add vinegar, salt and black pepper; cook 2 minutes or until liquid has evaporated. Serve warm or at room temperature.

Makes 6 to 8 servings

RED PEPPER CROSTINI: Brush thin slices of French bread with olive oil. Place on baking sheet; bake in preheated 350°F oven 10 minutes or until golden brown. Top with Red Pepper Antipasto.

CAPONATA

- 1 medium eggplant (about 1 pound), peeled and cut into ½-inch pieces
- 1 can (about 14 ounces) diced Italian plum tomatoes
- 1 onion, chopped
- 1 red bell pepper, cut into ½-inch pieces
- ½ cup salsa
- ¼ cup olive oil
- 2 tablespoons capers, drained
- 2 tablespoons balsamic vinegar
- 3 cloves garlic, minced
- 1 teaspoon dried oregano
- ¼ teaspoon salt
- ⅓ cup packed fresh basil leaves, cut into thin strips

  Toasted Italian or French bread slices

Slow Cooker Directions

1. Combine eggplant, tomatoes, onion, bell pepper, salsa, oil, capers, vinegar, garlic, oregano and salt in slow cooker.

2. Cover; cook on LOW 7 to 8 hours. Stir in basil. Serve at room temperature on bread slices.

Makes about 5 cups

MEDITERRANEAN FLATBREAD

  2 tablespoons olive oil, divided
½ cup thinly sliced yellow onion
½ cup thinly sliced red
    bell pepper
½ cup thinly sliced green
    bell pepper
  1 package (11 ounces)
    refrigerated French
    bread dough
  2 cloves garlic, minced
½ teaspoon dried rosemary
⅛ teaspoon red pepper flakes
    (optional)
⅓ cup coarsely chopped pitted
    kalamata olives
¼ cup grated Parmesan cheese

1. Preheat oven to 350°F.

2. Heat 1 tablespoon oil in large skillet over medium-high heat. Add onion and bell peppers; cook and stir 5 minutes or until onion begins to brown. Remove from heat.

3. Unroll dough on nonstick baking sheet. Combine garlic and remaining 1 tablespoon oil in small bowl; brush over dough. Sprinkle with rosemary and red pepper flakes, if desired. Top with onion mixture; sprinkle with olives.

4. Bake 16 to 18 minutes or until golden brown. Sprinkle with Parmesan. Remove to wire rack to cool slightly. Cut flatbread in half lengthwise; cut crosswise into 1-inch-wide strips.

Makes 16 pieces

PARTY CHEESE SPREAD

1 cup ricotta cheese

6 ounces cream cheese, softened

1 medium onion, chopped

2 tablespoons grated Parmesan cheese

1 tablespoon capers, rinsed and drained

2 anchovy fillets, mashed *or* 2 teaspoons anchovy paste

1 teaspoon dry mustard

1 teaspoon paprika

½ teaspoon hot pepper sauce

Red cabbage or bell pepper

Assorted cut-up vegetables and/or crackers

1. Beat ricotta cheese and cream cheese in large bowl with electric mixer at medium speed 3 to 5 minutes or until well blended.

2. Add onion, Parmesan, capers, anchovies, mustard, paprika and hot pepper sauce; mix well. Cover and refrigerate at least 1 day or up to 1 week to allow flavors to blend.

3. Just before serving, remove and discard any damaged outer leaves from cabbage. Slice small piece from bottom so cabbage will sit flat. Cut out inside portion of cabbage, leaving 1-inch-thick shell, being careful not to cut through bottom of cabbage. (Reserve inside of cabbage for another use.)

4. Spoon cheese spread into hollowed-out cabbage. Serve with vegetables.

Makes about 2 cups

GOAT CHEESE, CARAMELIZED ONION AND PROSCIUTTO FLATBREAD

2 tablespoons olive oil, plus additional for drizzling

1 large onion, sliced

¼ teaspoon salt

¼ cup water

1 package (about 14 ounces) refrigerated pizza dough

2 ounces goat cheese

4 slices prosciutto

½ teaspoon fresh thyme

1. Preheat oven to 450°F. Line baking sheet with parchment paper.

2. Heat 2 tablespoons oil in large skillet over medium heat. Add onion and salt; cook 18 to 20 minutes or until deep golden brown stirring occasionally and adding water halfway through cooking.

3. Roll out dough into two 9×5-inch rectangles on lightly floured surface. Transfer dough to prepared baking sheet; top with onion, goat cheese and prosciutto.

4. Bake 12 minutes or until crust is golden brown and prosciutto is crisp.

5. Drizzle with additional oil; sprinkle with thyme. Cut each flatbread into 12 pieces.

Makes 6 servings

VEGETABLE-TOPPED HUMMUS

1 can (about 15 ounces) chickpeas, rinsed and drained

2 tablespoons tahini

2 tablespoons lemon juice

1 clove garlic

¾ teaspoon salt

1 tomato, finely chopped

2 green onions, finely chopped

2 tablespoons chopped fresh parsley

Pita bread wedges or assorted crackers (optional)

1. Combine chickpeas, tahini, lemon juice, garlic and salt in food processor or blender; process until smooth.

2. Combine tomato, green onions and parsley in small bowl; stir gently to blend.

3. Spoon hummus into serving bowl; top with tomato mixture. Serve with pita, if desired.

Makes 8 servings

SIMPLE BRUSCHETTA

1 tablespoon olive oil

2 tablespoons thinly sliced red onion

1 clove garlic, minced

1 cup chopped seeded tomato

¼ teaspoon salt

⅛ teaspoon black pepper

Toasted or grilled baguette slices

¼ cup slivered fresh basil

1. Heat oil in medium skillet over medium heat. Add onion; cook and stir 3 minutes. Add garlic; cook and stir 1 minute.

2. Stir in tomatoes, salt and pepper; let stand 10 minutes. Serve mixture on baguette slices; sprinkle with basil.

Makes 4 servings

GLOBAL FLAVORS

MARGHERITA PANINI BITES

1 loaf (16 ounces) ciabatta or crusty Italian bread, cut into 16 (½-inch) slices

8 teaspoons pesto sauce

16 fresh basil leaves

8 slices mozzarella cheese

24 thin slices plum tomato (about 3 tomatoes)

Olive oil

1. Preheat grill or broiler. Spread one side of 8 bread slices with 1 teaspoon pesto. Top with 2 basil leaves, 1 mozzarella slice, 3 tomato slices and remaining bread slices.

2. Brush both sides of sandwiches lightly with oil. Grill sandwiches 5 minutes or until lightly browned and cheese is melted, turning once.

3. Cut each sandwich into quarters. Serve warm.

Makes 32 panini bites

TIPSY CHICKEN WRAPS

1 tablespoon dark sesame oil

1 pound ground chicken

8 ounces firm tofu, diced

½ red bell pepper, diced

3 green onions, sliced

1 tablespoon minced
   fresh ginger

2 cloves garlic, minced

½ cup Asian beer

⅓ cup hoisin sauce

1 teaspoon hot chili paste

½ cup chopped peanuts

2 heads Boston lettuce,
   separated into large leaves

   Whole fresh chives

1. Heat oil in large skillet over medium heat. Add chicken; cook until browned, stirring to break up meat.

2. Add tofu, bell pepper, green onions, ginger and garlic; cook and stir until green onions are softened. Add beer, hoisin sauce and chili paste; cook and stir until heated through. Stir in peanuts.

3. Place spoonful of chicken mixture in center of each lettuce leaf; roll up to enclose filling. Serve immediately.

Makes about 20 wraps

SERVING SUGGESTION: Wrap chives around filled leaves and tie to secure.

CRAB CAKES CANTON

7 ounces fresh, frozen or pasteurized crabmeat or imitation crabmeat

1½ cups fresh whole wheat bread crumbs (about 3 slices bread)

¼ cup thinly sliced green onions

1 clove garlic, minced

1 teaspoon minced fresh ginger

2 egg whites, lightly beaten

1 tablespoon teriyaki sauce

2 teaspoons vegetable oil

Prepared sweet and sour sauce (optional)

1. Pick out and discard any shell or cartilage from crabmeat.

2. Combine crabmeat, bread crumbs, green onions, garlic and ginger in medium bowl. Add egg whites and teriyaki sauce; mix well. Shape mixture into patties about ½ inch thick and 2 inches in diameter.*

3. Heat 1 teaspoon oil in large nonstick skillet over medium heat. Add half of crab cakes to skillet; cook 2 minutes per side or until golden brown. Remove to plate; keep warm. Repeat with remaining 1 teaspoon oil and crab cakes. Serve with sweet and sour sauce, if desired.

Makes 6 servings

*Crab cakes may be made ahead to this point; cover and refrigerate up to 24 hours before cooking.

THAI COFFEE CHICKEN SKEWERS

1¼ pounds chicken tenders, cut crosswise into ½-inch-wide strips

⅓ cup soy sauce

¼ cup strong brewed coffee

2 tablespoons plus 2 teaspoons lime juice, divided

4 cloves garlic, minced, divided

1 tablespoon plus 1 teaspoon minced fresh ginger, divided

½ teaspoon sriracha or hot chili sauce, divided

½ cup water

¼ cup hoisin sauce

2 tablespoons creamy peanut butter

1 tablespoon tomato paste

1 teaspoon sugar

4 green onions, cut into 1-inch pieces

1. Combine chicken, soy sauce, coffee, 2 tablespoons lime juice, 2 cloves garlic, 1 teaspoon ginger and ¼ teaspoon sriracha in large resealable food storage bag. Seal bag; shake well to coat. Marinate in refrigerator 1 to 2 hours.

2. Combine water, hoisin sauce, peanut butter, tomato paste, sugar, remaining 1 tablespoon ginger, 2 cloves garlic, 2 teaspoons lime juice and ¼ teaspoon sriracha sauce in medium bowl; mix well.

3. Soak eight 12-inch wooden skewers in water 30 minutes. Prepare grill for direct cooking.

4. Remove chicken from marinade; discard marinade. Alternately thread chicken and green onions onto skewers.

5. Grill skewers over medium heat 6 to 8 minutes or until chicken is cooked through, turning once. Serve with peanut sauce.

Makes 8 skewers

BEER BATTER TEMPURA

1½ cups all-purpose flour

1½ cups Japanese beer, chilled

1 teaspoon salt

  Dipping Sauce
    (recipe follows)

  Vegetable oil for frying

8 ounces green beans or
    asparagus tips

1 large sweet potato, cut
    into ¼-inch slices

1 medium eggplant, cut
    into ¼-inch slices

1. Combine flour, beer and salt in medium bowl just until blended. Batter should be thin and lumpy. *Do not overmix.* Let stand 15 minutes. Meanwhile, prepare Dipping Sauce.

2. Heat 1 inch of oil in large saucepan to 375°F; adjust heat to maintain temperature.

3. Dip 10 to 12 green beans in batter; add to hot oil. Fry until light golden brown. Remove with slotted spoon; drain on wire racks or paper towel-lined plate. Repeat with remaining vegetables, working with only one vegetable at a time and being careful not to crowd vegetables. Serve with Dipping Sauce.

Makes 4 servings

DIPPING SAUCE

½ cup soy sauce

2 tablespoons rice wine

1 tablespoon sugar

½ teaspoon white vinegar

2 teaspoons minced fresh ginger

1 clove garlic, minced

2 green onions, thinly sliced

Combine soy sauce, rice wine, sugar and vinegar in small saucepan; cook and stir over medium heat 3 minutes or until sugar dissolves. Add ginger and garlic; cook 2 minutes. Stir in green onions; remove from heat.

Makes about 1 cup

SPICY KOREAN CHICKEN WINGS

2 tablespoons peanut oil,
  plus additional for frying

2 tablespoons grated
  fresh ginger

½ cup reduced-sodium
  soy sauce

¼ cup cider vinegar

¼ cup honey

¼ cup chili garlic sauce

2 tablespoons orange juice

1 tablespoon sesame oil

18 chicken wings or
  drummettes

  Sesame seeds (optional)

1. Heat 2 tablespoons peanut oil in medium skillet over medium-high heat. Add ginger; cook and stir 1 minute. Add soy sauce, vinegar, honey, chili garlic sauce, orange juice and sesame oil; cook and stir 2 minutes.

2. Heat 2 inches of peanut oil in large heavy saucepan over medium-high heat to 350° to 375°F; adjust heat to maintain temperature.

3. Rinse wings under cold water; pat dry with paper towels. Remove and discard wing tips.

4. Add wings to oil; cook 8 to 10 minutes or until crispy, browned and cooked through. Remove with slotted spoon to paper towel-lined plate.

5. Add wings to sauce; toss to coat. Sprinkle with sesame seeds, if desired.

Makes 6 to 8 servings

CAPER-RICE CROQUETTES

⅔ cup water

⅓ cup uncooked rice

2 ounces prosciutto slices, finely chopped

1 egg yolk, beaten

1 tablespoons capers, rinsed and drained

⅛ teaspoon salt

⅛ teaspoon dried oregano

⅛ teaspoon black pepper

⅔ cup fresh bread crumbs

1 to 1½ tablespoons butter

1 tablespoon olive oil

1. Bring water to a boil in small saucepan over high heat. Stir in rice. Reduce heat to low; cover and simmer about 14 minutes or until rice is tender and water has been absorbed. Transfer rice to medium bowl; cool until almost room temperature.

2. Add prosciutto, egg yolk, capers, salt, oregano and pepper; mix well. Spread bread crumbs on large plate. Shape rice mixture into 18 (1¼-inch) balls. Flatten slightly; gently coat with bread crumbs. Place on plate; refrigerate 15 to 30 minutes or until firm.

3. Heat 1 tablespoon butter and oil in large heavy skillet over medium-high heat until butter melts. Add half of croquettes to skillet; cook 2 to 3 minutes or until golden brown. Turn and cook 1 to 2 minutes or until golden brown. Remove to plate; keep warm. Repeat with remaining croquettes, adding remaining butter if necessary. Serve hot.

Makes 6 servings

CRAB RANGOON WITH SPICY DIPPING SAUCE

1 cup ketchup

¼ cup chili garlic sauce

4 teaspoons Chinese
   hot mustard

1 package (8 ounces)
   cream cheese, softened

1 can (6 ounces) lump
   crabmeat, well drained

⅓ cup minced green onions

1 package (12 ounces)
   wonton wrappers

1 egg white, beaten

   Vegetable oil for frying

1. Combine ketchup, chili garlic sauce and mustard in small bowl; mix well.

2. Beat cream cheese in medium bowl with electric mixer at medium speed until light and fluffy. Stir in crabmeat and green onions.

3. Arrange wonton wrappers on clean work surface. Place 1 rounded teaspoon crab mixture in center of each wrapper. Brush inside edges with egg white. Fold in half diagonally to form triangle; press edges firmly to seal.

4. Heat 2 inches of oil in deep heavy saucepan over medium-high heat to 350°F; adjust heat to maintain temperature. Fry wontons in batches 2 minutes per side or until golden brown. Remove with slotted spoon to paper towel-lined plate. Serve immediately with dipping sauce.

Makes about 12 servings (44 wontons)

VARIATION: Crab Rangoon can be baked instead of fried, but the results will not be as crisp or as golden in color. Prepare as directed through step 3, then arrange triangles 1 inch apart on parchment-lined baking sheets. Spray tops of triangles with nonstick cooking spray. Bake in preheated 375°F oven about 11 minutes or until lightly browned. Serve immediately.

MOZZARELLA IN CARROZZA

  2 **eggs**

⅓ **cup milk**

¼ **teaspoon salt**

⅛ **teaspoon black pepper**

  8 **slices country Italian bread**

  6 **ounces fresh mozzarella, cut into ¼-inch slices**

  8 **oil-packed sun-dried tomatoes, drained and cut into strips**

  8 **to 12 fresh basil leaves, torn**

1½ **tablespoons olive oil**

1. Whisk eggs, milk, salt and pepper in shallow bowl or baking dish until well blended.

2. Place 4 bread slices on work surface. Top with mozzarella, sun-dried tomatoes, basil and remaining bread slices.

3. Heat oil in large skillet over medium heat. Dip sandwiches in egg mixture, turning and pressing to coat completely. Add sandwiches to skillet; cook about 5 minutes per side or until golden brown. Cut into strips or squares.

Makes about 8 appetizer servings

TIP: To serve these sandwiches as a snack or lunch instead of an appetizer, cut them in half instead of squares.

BACON-WRAPPED TERIYAKI SHRIMP

1 pound large raw shrimp, peeled and deveined (with tails on)

¼ cup teriyaki marinade

11 to 12 slices bacon, cut in half crosswise

1. Preheat oven to 425°F. Line shallow baking pan with foil.

2. Place shrimp in large resealable food storage bag. Add teriyaki marinade; seal bag and turn to coat. Marinate in refrigerator 15 to 20 minutes.

3. Remove shrimp from bag; reserve marinade. Wrap each shrimp with one piece bacon. Place in prepared pan; brush bacon with some of reserved marinade.

4. Bake 15 minutes or until bacon is crisp and shrimp are pink and opaque.

Makes 4 servings

TIP: Do not use thick-cut bacon for this recipe, as the bacon will not be completely cooked when the shrimp are done.

FRIED CALAMARI WITH TARTAR SAUCE

Tartar Sauce
  (recipe follows)
1 pound cleaned squid
  (body tubes, tentacles
  or a combination),
  rinsed and patted dry
¾ cup plain dry bread crumbs
1 egg
1 tablespoon milk
  Vegetable oil
  Lemon wedges (optional)

1. Prepare Tartar Sauce; set aside. Line large baking sheet with waxed paper. Cut squid into ¼-inch rings.

2. Place bread crumbs in medium bowl. Beat egg and milk in separate medium bowl. Add squid; stir to coat. Transfer squid to bowl with bread crumbs; toss to coat. Place on prepared baking sheet. Refrigerate 15 minutes.

3. Heat 1½ inches of oil in large heavy saucepan over medium-high heat to 350°F; adjust heat to maintain temperature.* Fry squid in batches, 8 to 10 pieces at a time, 45 seconds or until golden brown. (Squid will pop and spatter during frying; do not stand too close to saucepan.) *Do not overcook squid or it will become tough.* Remove with slotted spoon to paper towel-lined plate.

4. Serve immediately with Tartar Sauce and lemon wedges, if desired.

Makes 2 to 3 servings

To shallow fry squid, heat about ¼ inch of oil in large skillet over medium-high heat; reduce heat to medium. Add single layer of squid to oil without crowding. Cook 1 minute per side or until golden brown. Drain on paper towel-lined plate.

TARTAR SAUCE: Combine 1⅓ cups mayonnaise, 2 tablespoons chopped fresh Italian parsley, 1 thinly sliced green onion, 1 tablespoon minced drained capers and 1 minced small sweet gherkin or pickle in medium bowl; mix well. Cover and refrigerate until ready to serve.

MEDITERRANEAN FRITTATA

¼ cup extra virgin olive oil

5 small onions, thinly sliced

1 can (about 14 ounces) whole tomatoes, drained and chopped

4 ounces prosciutto or cooked ham, chopped

¼ cup grated Parmesan cheese

2 tablespoons chopped fresh parsley

½ teaspoon dried marjoram

¼ teaspoon salt

¼ teaspoon dried basil

⅛ teaspoon black pepper

6 eggs

2 tablespoons butter

1. Heat oil in large skillet over medium-high heat. Add onions; cook and stir 8 to 10 minutes or until soft and golden. Reduce heat to medium. Add tomatoes; cook 5 minutes. Remove vegetables to large bowl with slotted spoon; discard drippings. Cool to room temperature.

2. Add prosciutto, Parmesan, parsley, marjoram, salt, basil and pepper to tomato mixture; mix well. Whisk eggs in medium bowl; stir into prosciutto mixture.

3. Preheat broiler. Heat butter in medium broilerproof skillet over medium heat until melted and bubbly. Reduce heat to low. Add egg mixture to skillet, spreading evenly. Cook 8 to 10 minutes until all but top ¼ inch of frittata is set. (Shake pan gently to test.) *Do not stir.*

4. Broil frittata about 4 inches from heat 1 to 2 minutes or until top is set. (Do not brown or frittata will be dry.) Serve warm or at room temperature.

Makes 6 to 8 appetizer servings

ASIAN BARBECUE SKEWERS

2 pounds boneless skinless
  chicken thighs

½ cup soy sauce

⅓ cup packed brown sugar

2 tablespoons sesame oil

3 cloves garlic, minced

½ cup thinly sliced
  green onions

1 tablespoon toasted
  sesame seeds (optional)

Slow Cooker Directions

1. Cut each thigh into four pieces about 1½ inches thick. Thread chicken onto 7-inch wooden skewers, folding thinner pieces, if necessary. Place skewers in slow cooker, layering as flat as possible.

2. Combine soy sauce, brown sugar, oil and garlic in small bowl; mix well. Reserve ⅓ cup sauce; pour remaining sauce over skewers.

3. Cover; cook on LOW 2 hours. Turn skewers and cook on LOW 1 hour.

4. Transfer skewers to serving platter. Discard cooking liquid. Pour reserved sauce over skewers; sprinkle with green onions and sesame seeds, if desired.

Makes 4 to 6 servings

MARINATED ANTIPASTO

- ¼ cup extra virgin olive oil
- 2 tablespoons balsamic vinegar
- 1 clove garlic, minced
- ½ teaspoon sugar
- ½ teaspoon salt
- ¼ teaspoon black pepper
- 1 pint (2 cups) cherry tomatoes
- 1 can (about 14 ounces) quartered artichoke hearts, drained
- 8 ounces small balls or cubes fresh mozzarella
- 1 cup drained pitted kalamata olives
- ¼ cup slivered fresh basil

  Lettuce leaves

1. Combine oil, vinegar, garlic, sugar, salt and pepper in medium bowl; mix well. Add tomatoes, artichokes, mozzarella, olives and basil; toss to coat. Let stand at room temperature 30 minutes.

2. Line platter with lettuce. Arrange antipasto over lettuce; serve at room temperature.

Makes about 5 cups

SERVING SUGGESTION: Serve antipasto with toothpicks as an appetizer or spoon over Bibb lettuce leaves for a first-course salad.

LEMON AND GARLIC SHRIMP

¼ cup olive oil

2 tablespoons butter

1 pound large raw shrimp, peeled and deveined (with tails on)

3 cloves garlic, crushed

2 tablespoons lemon juice

½ teaspoon paprika

¼ teaspoon salt

Black pepper

2 tablespoons chopped fresh Italian parsley

French or Italian bread slices

1. Heat oil and butter in large skillet over medium-high heat until butter melts and mixture sizzles. Add shrimp and garlic; cook and stir 4 to 5 minutes until shrimp are pink and opaque.

2. Add lemon juice, paprika, salt and pepper; cook and stir 1 minute. Remove from heat; discard garlic.

3. Spoon shrimp and skillet juices into large serving bowl; sprinkle with parsley. Serve with bread for dipping.

Makes 6 to 8 servings

ACKNOWLEDGMENTS

The publisher would like to thank the companies and organizations listed below for the use of their recipes and photographs in this publication.

Campbell Soup Company

Dole Food Company, Inc.

Florida Department of Citrus

METRIC CONVERSION CHART

VOLUME MEASUREMENTS (dry)

$\frac{1}{8}$ teaspoon = 0.5 mL
$\frac{1}{4}$ teaspoon = 1 mL
$\frac{1}{2}$ teaspoon = 2 mL
$\frac{3}{4}$ teaspoon = 4 mL
1 teaspoon = 5 mL
1 tablespoon = 15 mL
2 tablespoons = 30 mL
$\frac{1}{4}$ cup = 60 mL
$\frac{1}{3}$ cup = 75 mL
$\frac{1}{2}$ cup = 125 mL
$\frac{2}{3}$ cup = 150 mL
$\frac{3}{4}$ cup = 175 mL
1 cup = 250 mL
2 cups = 1 pint = 500 mL
3 cups = 750 mL
4 cups = 1 quart = 1 L

VOLUME MEASUREMENTS (fluid)

1 fluid ounce (2 tablespoons) = 30 mL
4 fluid ounces ($\frac{1}{2}$ cup) = 125 mL
8 fluid ounces (1 cup) = 250 mL
12 fluid ounces (1$\frac{1}{2}$ cups) = 375 mL
16 fluid ounces (2 cups) = 500 mL

WEIGHTS (mass)

$\frac{1}{2}$ ounce = 15 g
1 ounce = 30 g
3 ounces = 90 g
4 ounces = 120 g
8 ounces = 225 g
10 ounces = 285 g
12 ounces = 360 g
16 ounces = 1 pound = 450 g

DIMENSIONS

$\frac{1}{16}$ inch = 2 mm
$\frac{1}{8}$ inch = 3 mm
$\frac{1}{4}$ inch = 6 mm
$\frac{1}{2}$ inch = 1.5 cm
$\frac{3}{4}$ inch = 2 cm
1 inch = 2.5 cm

OVEN TEMPERATURES

250°F = 120°C
275°F = 140°C
300°F = 150°C
325°F = 160°C
350°F = 180°C
375°F = 190°C
400°F = 200°C
425°F = 220°C
450°F = 230°C

BAKING PAN SIZES

Utensil	Size in Inches/Quarts	Metric Volume	Size in Centimeters
Baking or Cake Pan (square or rectangular)	8×8×2	2 L	20×20×5
	9×9×2	2.5 L	23×23×5
	12×8×2	3 L	30×20×5
	13×9×2	3.5 L	33×23×5
Loaf Pan	8×4×3	1.5 L	20×10×7
	9×5×3	2 L	23×13×7
Round Layer Cake Pan	8×1½	1.2 L	20×4
	9×1½	1.5 L	23×4
Pie Plate	8×1¼	750 mL	20×3
	9×1¼	1 L	23×3
Baking Dish or Casserole	1 quart	1 L	—
	1½ quart	1.5 L	—
	2 quart	2 L	—